WRITING AND ART GO HAND IN HAND

To Teach Language Skills

by
Diane M. Bonica

Incentive Publications, Inc.
Nashville, Tennessee

Acknowledgments
To Afton, Beverly, Enid and Ona . . .
the encouraging force that spurred me onward.

Illustrated by Angela Cravens Wilson
Cover by Susan Eaddy
Edited by Jennifer Goodman
and Sally Sharpe

ISBN 0-86530-068-2

Table of Contents

SPRING

SUMMER

HOLIDAYS

INTRODUCTION

WRITING AND ART GO HAND IN HAND will fill the needs of teachers who wish to pack the school year with creative writing experiences. The procedural presentation of this book is intended to reduce teacher preparation in order to increase the students' exposure to writing as well as to develop each student's writing proficiency. It is generally true that once a child has had a successful writing experience, the child will look forward to the chance to write again. By combining writing activities and creative art projects, this book offers students positive experiences. Moreover, each lesson is structured around a poetic verse form, teaching the students as much as a week's worth of language skills!

A wide variety of poetic forms and styles is presented in this book in order to meet the needs and abilities of students at different grade levels. Even students in kindergarten can learn to "write" creatively with a teacher, parent, or upper-grade student acting as a scribe.

I invite you to explore this book and discover for yourself the exciting experiences awaiting your students. Study the various poetic forms and feel free to invent your own. Review the art projects that accompany each lesson and consider them as viable means for presenting the writing activities. WRITING AND ART GO HAND IN HAND will help to develop within your classroom an energy that will result in personal accomplishment and pleasure. Choose an activity now and open wide the door to creative endeavors!

Diane M. Bonica

TWELVE POETIC TECHNIQUES

Alliteration

READY

Alliteration is achieved by combining several words with the same initial sound. The words may be written in sentence or verse form. In either case, alliterative energy is contagious, making alliteration a fine activity for beginning writers.

SET

Select a letter of the alphabet. Help the class brainstorm to make a list of words beginning with this letter.

WRITE

Have each student write an alliterative verse about an imaginary person whose name begins with the chosen letter. Instruct the students to continue writing until they cannot think of any more words.

> *Barney Buff bought bright blue baseballs.*
> *When Barney Buff batted, his bright blue*
> *baseballs burst! Boo, boo, boo!*

PRESENT

Make a large cutout of the chosen letter for each student. Let the students copy their poems on the letters. Display the letters for all to see.

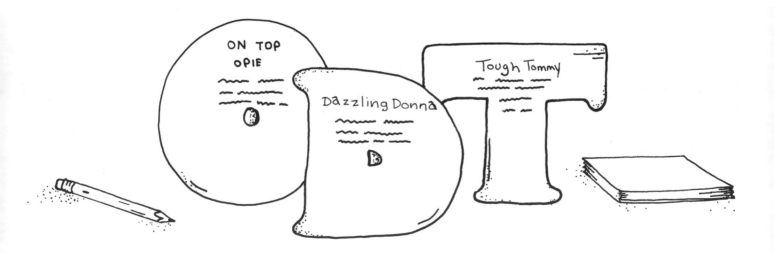

Simile

READY

A simile is a device used in comparative statements which is easily recognized by the words like or as.

SET

Building a simile is a simple process when aided by a model.

(topic)	is as	(adjective)	as	(comparative noun)
brown	is as	prickly	as	pine cones

To build similes in class, select a color and brainstorm all of its characteristics (the adjective column). Write all ideas on the chalkboard for easy reference.

WRITE

Instruct the students to write as many comparisons as possible. The combination of three or more similes makes a nice product.

blue is...
as clear as water
as bright as day
as deep as oceans

brown is...
as cool as shade
as foamy as root beer
as gritty as sand

PRESENT

Have the students copy their color similes on square construction paper sheets of the same colors as the simile colors. Each student may run two yarn loops through the square and insert a stick through the loops to make a flag or banner. A variety of colors makes an attractive display.

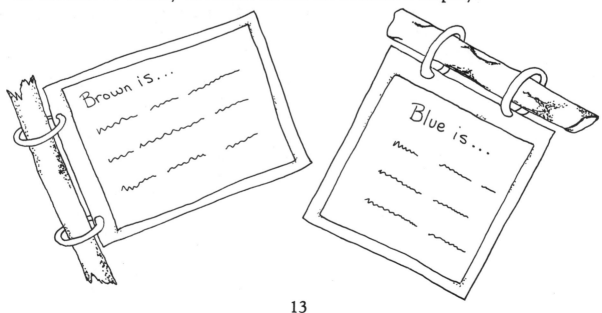

Metaphor

READY

A metaphor is a comparative device used to link two objects that often appear to have very little in common. The beauty of a metaphor is that the poet is free to do the convincing. Even the youngest poet will love this writing activity.

SET

Select a topic and brainstorm every aspect of it. Explore sense words for sights, smells, sounds, tastes, and touches. Now, brainstorm other words that share a common characteristic with the chosen topic.

> Night is black.
> Soot, smoke, and ink are black.

WRITE

Have each child choose his or her own comparison and enlarge it by adding lines that will make the image real.

> *Night is a chimney*
> *smoking, flaring*
> *pushing its blackness over all the earth.*

> *Night is a giant leopard*
> *stalking the earth*
> *with its incredible speed.*

PRESENT

The class may illustrate their metaphors with ripped paper artwork. (All of the figures in the illustration are ripped from paper...without using scissors.) Have the students copy their poems below their artwork or on clean sheets of paper.

Cinquain

READY

A cinquain is a verse of five lines following the pattern of (1,2,3,4,1) words in each line. A cinquain produces a fragile image or a delicate thought. This activity appears difficult, but the pattern makes it easy . . . even for beginners!

SET

Explore the poem pattern with the class by helping them write several practice poems.

line 1	title	(noun)
line 2	description of title	(2 adj.)
line 3	action of title	(3 verbs)
line 4	statement or feeling	(4-word phrase)
line 5	repeated title or synonym	(noun)

WRITE

Display the poem model or give a copy of the model to each child. Have each student select a subject for a poem and brainstorm all words that could be used in the poem. Instruct each student to write and revise a cinquain.

winter
icy, cold
piercing, chilling, freezing
changing greenness into white
winter

PRESENT

Display the cinquains by mounting them on chalk backgrounds of muted hues. Give each student a 5" x 7" sheet of white paper. Direct the students to color patches on their papers with several colors of chalk and to rub the papers with tissue to combine the colors. Have the students copy their poems on the chalk papers with black ink.

Diamante'

READY

A diamante', a poem form which derives its name from its diamond shape, expresses a sharp contrast between two opposite themes. This type of verse involves a knowledge of the parts of speech and thus is best suited for upper-grade students.

SET

Begin the writing activity with a brainstorming session on antonyms. Because nature is full of opposing forces, topics drawn from nature offer great possibilities.

WRITE

Have the class carefully study the diamante' form below before they begin writing. The fourth line is crucial because it is here that the transition from the description of the theme to its opposite begins. Instruct each student to write a diamanté about some aspect of nature.

line 1	*jungle*	(topic)
line 2	*abundant, soggy*	(2 adj.)
line 3	*growing, stretching, living*	(3 "ing" verbs)
line 4	*vegetation, overgrowth, void, wasteland*	(2 nouns/ 2 nouns)
line 5	*decaying, drying, dying*	(3 "ing" verbs)
line 6	*desert*	(opposite)

PRESENT

To accentuate the opposing ideas expressed in this type of verse, have the students make positive/negative backdrops for their poems. Instruct each student to fold a sheet of white paper in half and to carefully cut a design out of a sheet of black paper to make a positive cutout and a negative stencil. Each student should paste the positive cutout on half of the white page and the negative stencil on the other half. Have the students copy their poems on their designs.

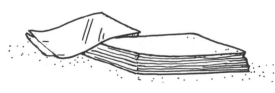

16

Haiku

READY

A haiku, an oriental verse form containing 17 syllables, is organized into three lines of (5,7,5) syllables each. Nature's wonder is the haiku's theme.

SET

Preparation for writing haiku should involve exposure to published haiku verse. One must appreciate the quality and meter of the haiku before attempting to write a haiku.

WRITE

Reproduce a copy of the haiku form for each student. Instruct each student to write a haiku.

"Rosebud"

line 1	*Such precious beauty*	(5 syllables)
line 2	*Upon a stalk so fearsome*	(7 syllables)
line 3	*How wise is nature!*	(5 syllables)

To help students choose themes, supply the class with nature pictures or allow the students to write their poems outdoors.

PRESENT

Have each student cut a sheet of white paper to 4½" x 12" size. Instruct the students to "splatter paint" prints in delicate hues on their papers. The students may copy their poems on the papers with black ink after the paint has dried.

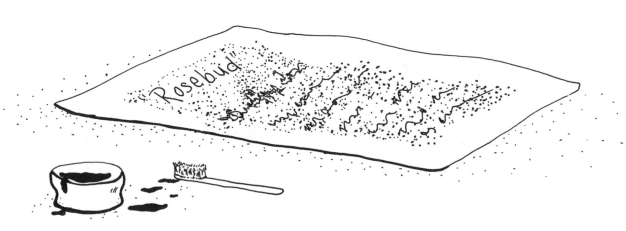

Quintet

READY

A quintet is syllabic verse of five lines that tells a story. The syllable pattern is (3,5,7,9,3) for each line respectively. A quintet brings a visual image alive. Upper-grade students will enjoy the quintet challenge.

SET

Nature photographs provide an excellent springboard for quintet writing. Display several nature photos for the students to use as sources for quintet themes.

WRITE

Distribute a quintet poem model to each student. Spend class time creating a few examples.

line 1	*during fall*	(when, 3 syl.)
line 2	*deep inside the woods*	(where, 5 syl.)
line 3	*busy squirrels rush about*	(what, 7 syl.)
line 4	*gathering nuts and berries galore*	(activity, 9 syl.)
line 5	*winter feast*	(thought, 3 syl.)

PRESENT

Let the students make owls to accompany their nature quintets. Using a pretzel, a pine cone, paper and glue, each student may construct an owl like the one below. Display the poems and owls together.

Couplet

READY

A couplet is two lines of rhymed verse with the rhyme pattern (a, a). A couplet can be short or long, but it must always rhyme.

SET

Select a broad theme and have the class brainstorm for rhyming words that could be used in a couplet.

WRITE

Instruct each student to choose a theme and write a couplet. Remind the students that because a couplet has no set meter, the rhyme is most important.

"Spring"

About spring
I'll sing

"Spring"

What I like about the spring
is every single little thing

Couplets can be combined to form poems of four, six, twelve or more lines.

PRESENT

To emphasize the "linking quality" of a couplet, have the students write each line of their original poems on strips of 2½" x 6" paper. Each student may join his or her strips together to make a paper chain.

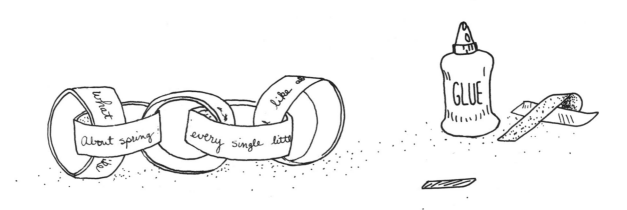

Tercet

READY

A tercet is a rhymed or unrhymed poem of three lines. Tercets may have light and flowing rhyme patterns which are suitable for even the youngest of authors.

SET

You may simplify the process of introducing the class to rhyme patterns by using visual models. The tercet may follow any of the patterns below. (Like letters indicate rhyming words.)

_____ a	_____ a	_____ a
_____ a	_____ b	_____ b
_____ a	_____ a	_____ b

WRITE

Animals make fine themes for tercets. Select three to five animals and have the class brainstorm to make a list of rhyming words. Instruct each student to write a tercet about one of the selected animals.

"The Bird"

A yellow bird   (a)
Can sing a song   (b)
Without a word   (a)

PRESENT

Potato-print backgrounds provide an excellent publication mode for animal tercets. Give each child half of a potato and instruct the student to carve his or her chosen animal in the end of the potato. Direct the students to dip their potatoes in tempera paint and then press their potatoes all over sheets of construction paper. When the paint dries, the students may copy their poems on their printed papers.

Quatrain

READY

The quatrain, a very popular rhymed verse form used in most elementary schools, is a poem of four lines which follows several rhyme patterns. The quatrain is a light and sometimes humorous verse which is suited to the writing ability and temperament of young children.

SET

Read several quatrains found in existing literature to the class. (The most familiar sources are Mother Goose rhymes.) Display and discuss the various quatrain rhyme schemes. (Like letters indicate rhyming words.)

_____ a	_____ a	_____ a	_____ a
_____ b	_____ b	_____ a	_____ a
_____ a	_____ c	_____ b	_____ b
_____ b	_____ b	_____ a	_____ b

WRITE

Have the class brainstorm to make a "word bank" of rhyming words. Instruct each student to select a topic for a quatrain.

My favorite game is tennis,   (a)
I'm learning more each day.   (b)
My dad thinks I'm a menace,   (a)
When I hit the ball his way.   (b)

PRESENT

Have the students display their quatrains on shapes that emphasize the chosen themes. For example, poems with sports themes may be copied on shoe shapes cut from construction paper.

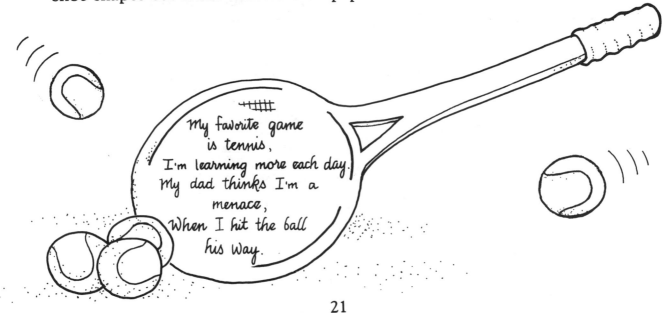

21

Limerick

READY

A limerick is a humorous verse form of five lines with the rhyme pattern (a,a,b,b,a). (A limerick does require some advanced writing skill.)

SET

Allow the students to read many limericks before starting this activity. Once the students are familiar with the meter, limerick writing may begin!

WRITE

This step-by-step approach to limerick writing will be helpful to students.

line 1 *There was an old man with a cane*
(state the situation)

line 2 *Who tried to do flips down the lane*
(what happened)

line 3 *But his cane somehow broke*
(what went wrong)

line 4 *And this sorry old bloke*
(what went wrong)

line 5 *Ended up with a terrible pain*
(result)

PRESENT

Advertising agencies often use limericks on billboards. Capitalize on this idea for a corresponding art project. Instruct the students to illustrate their limericks on poster board and to copy their poems on the posters in bold print.

Noun Verse

READY

A noun verse is a patterned poem of four lines. Each line requires a specific type of word. Noun verses are quick, pleasant poems that lend themselves to many subjects.

SET

Copy the noun verse pattern on the chalkboard or reproduce one copy of the pattern for each student. Discuss the pattern with the class and help them write several practice poems.

WRITE

Have each student select a theme and write a noun verse.

line 1	*butterflies*	(noun)
line 2	*delicate, graceful*	(2 adj.)
line 3	*floating, hovering*	(2 "ing" verbs)
line 4	*monarchs*	(synonym)

PRESENT

Using colored tissue paper, each student may make a multicolored backdrop for his or her noun verse. Have the student paste tissue pieces in overlapping patterns on sheets of construction paper. When the glue dries, the student may print his or her poem in the center of the paper.

AUTUMN

Leaves of Autumn

READY

Autumn leaves lend themselves well to metaphorical sketches. Have your class do this activity to "whirl" into fall.

SET

If a leaf could be something else, what would it be? Have the class brainstorm for answers to this question. Encourage the students to think of descriptive and active words as well as nouns. Write all suggestions on the board for easy reference.

WRITE

Prepare the class for writing metaphorical sketches by giving each student a copy of this model.

line 1   *autumn leaves are multicolored gliders*
          (state the comparison)

line 2   *floating, diving, flying*
          (describe the motion involved)

line 3   *they puncture clouds and fall gently to earth*
          (tell what happens or how you feel)

PRESENT

Let the students go outside to collect autumn leaves for crayon leaf rubbings. Each student may copy his or her poem on a leaf rubbing background.

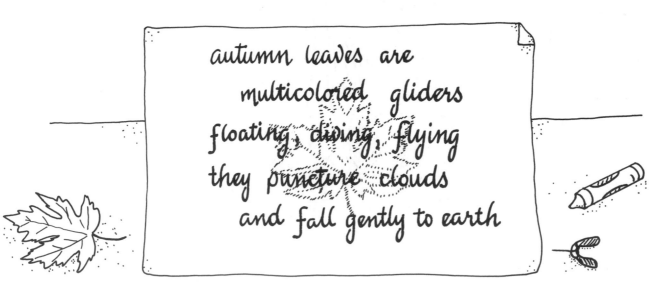

Fall Colors

READY

Magnificent color words add brilliant touches to fall poems. Send the class on an exciting color word hunt with this writing activity.

SET

Write the seven rainbow colors on the board. Have the class brainstorm to make a list of other color words for each rainbow color. The class will discover that red can be crimson, scarlet, cherry, ruby, or strawberry. Then have the class brainstorm to make a list of all of the things that can be seen in autumn (pumpkins, scarecrows, ripened fruit, falling leaves, seeds, blue skies, etc.).

WRITE

Older students may write in free verse to describe a color-filled autumn scene. Younger students may use the poem model below to write brilliant autumn verses.

line 1   My autumn eyes behold

lines 2-4   (color word)   (object)   (where it's seen)

My autumn eyes behold
Golden pumpkins on the vine
Lemon leaves blowing in the breeze
Red-streaked sunsets on the horizon

PRESENT

Have each student draw a large face with sunglasses on a large sheet of paper. Instruct each student to draw the autumn scene described in his or her poem on the lenses of the sunglasses. Display the poems and illustrations together.

My autumn eyes behold
Golden pumpkins on the vine
Lemon leaves blowing in the breeze
Red-streaked sunsets on the horizon

Scarecrow Selections

READY

Scarecrows, often called "guardians of the harvest", are perfect subjects for autumn verses.

SET

Begin an open discussion about fall and harvest time. Be sure to include all aspects of the bountiful season. End the discussion by talking about scarecrows. Mention the aromas, sights and sounds that a scarecrow might experience.

WRITE

Have the class write scarecrow poems using pensee' verse. Introduce the class to this new verse form with the model below.

line 1	the topic	(2 syllables)
line 2	a description	(4 syllables)
line 3	the action	(7 syllables)
line 4	the setting	(8 syllables)
line 5	a thought	(6 syllables)

Scarecrow
Stuffed man of straw
Looks upon fields of plenty
Where golden yellow corn grows tall
A brilliant fall display

PRESENT

Have the students make three-dimensional scarecrows on which to display their poems. Provide the class with raffia (commercial straw), fabric, trim, thread, needles, craft sticks, and Styrofoam bases. Demonstrate how to form straw into a scarecrow skeleton and how to make clothing and facial features with the other materials. The students may attach their scarecrows to craft sticks, anchor the sticks to Styrofoam bases, and attach their poems to the scarecrows. Display the straw figures around the room.

Fall Textures

READY

Fall not only delights the eyes with an array of beautiful colors, but it also stimulates all of the senses. Arouse the senses of every student with this descriptive writing activity.

SET

Have the class brainstorm to make a list of all fall characteristics (leaves, flowers, fruits, vegetables, weather tendencies, etc.).

WRITE

Let each student choose three autumn items and write a poem containing two descriptive words for each item. Help the students write their descriptive poems by displaying this model.

line 1   I like the feel of fall
lines 2-4   ("touch" adj.)   ("color" adj.)   (noun)

I like the feel of fall
Crunchy brown leaves
Prickly green grass
Fuzzy orange caterpillars

PRESENT

Supply the class with items of many different textures (fabrics, cotton, bark, leaves, etc.). Let the students experiment with texture as they glue items on construction paper to make autumn scenes. Display the poems and pictures together.

Apple Aroma

READY

Ripe apples are characteristic of autumn. Use this autumn specialty for a writing activity. Students will discover that apple themes abound with poetic possibilities.

SET

Ask each student to bring a ripe, red apple to class. After cutting each apple in half, permit the students to eat half of an apple. While the students are eating, lead a discussion about apples. Have the students suggest many descriptive words.

WRITE

Have each student write an apple poem using a cinquain format. Emphasize the importance of sharp descriptive words.

line 1	*apple*	(noun)
line 2	*scrumptious, delectable*	(2 adj.)
line 3	*crisping, oozing, crunching*	(3 "ing" verbs)
line 4	*offering fall's best treat*	(4-word phrase)
line 5	*delicious*	(1 word)

PRESENT

Display the apple cinquains amid aromatic prints. Pour red, green and yellow paint on Styrofoam plates. Have each student dip an apple half in paint and press the apple on a sheet of paper. After the paint dries, the students may copy their poems on their apple designs.

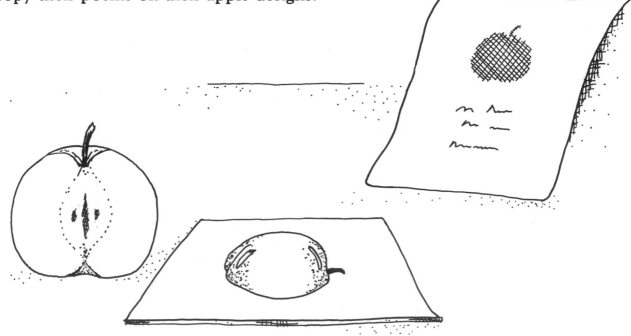

Selective Seed Study

READY

Fall winds scatter seeds everywhere. Because there are seeds of all shapes and sizes, a simile lends itself well to the comparative characteristics of seeds.

SET

Ask each student to bring a seed to class (watermelon seed, acorn, fruit pit, milkweed, pine cone, etc.). Display the seeds and discuss the characteristics of each with the class.

WRITE

Instruct the students to write descriptive similes about seeds. Provide the class with several examples.

My seed is as sharp as
the tip of my scissors,
the blade on a knife,
the point on a bull's horn.

My seed is as brown as
a cup of root beer,
a furry hamster,
a puddle of mud.

PRESENT

Have each student create a picture of his or her seed using paint, construction paper, markers, and other materials. Let each picture be as unique as each seed! Arrange the pictures and poems to make an interesting display.

Autumn Activity

READY

Autumn abounds with activity! School begins, football season arrives, harvest time commences, and many other festivities occur. Use the activity of fall as a springboard for a great writing activity.

SET

Ask the class to brainstorm to make a list of all of the activities of fall. Tell them to include activities of family members, friends, animals and nature.

WRITE

An easy "fill-in" poem model will help students write original "autumn activity" poems.

line 1	In autumn . . .
lines 2-4	(noun) (verb) (noun) (phrase)
line 5	and I (verb) (noun) (phrase)

In autumn...
squirrels gather nuts in the forest,
Mom cans peaches in the kitchen,
Davy plays football in the park,
and I do homework all afternoon.

PRESENT

The class can make stencil prints to use as backdrops for their poems. Instruct the students to cut Styrofoam trays to 4" x 2" dimensions. Using a pencil, each student may sketch an object or scene representative of a fall activity on the tray. (Remind them to press down hard to make indentions.) After brushing a layer of tempera paint over the design, each student may press the tray on a sheet of paper to make a print. When the paint is dry, the students may copy their poems on the prints.

Leaf Lullaby

READY

Autumn is the season during which many animals prepare for a long winter's sleep. Help the students write lullabies that will sooth the tumbling leaves preparing for a winter's rest.

SET

Bring several leaves to class and let them fall before the students. As a class, brainstorm all of the words that describe how the leaves descended to the floor. Talk about dreams and ask the students to imagine what kind of dream a leaf might have.

WRITE

Guide the students through the poem model and then ask them to write their own leaf lullabies.

line 1   Sleep,____(adj.)____ leaf, sleep!
line 2   (verb)_____ (adv.)_____ into your (adj.) bed.
line 3   Dream of _____ (what a leaf dreams of)_____.
line 4   Sleep,____(adj.)____ leaf, sleep!

Sleep, yellow leaf, sleep!
Tumble lightly into your autumn bed.
Dream of sunny days and warm weather.
Sleep, yellow leaf, sleep!

PRESENT

Give each student a leaf. Have the students place the leaves vein side up on their desks. After covering the leaf with white paper, each student may rub over the leaf with colored crayons. The students may cut out the leaf impressions and paste them on sheets of black construction paper. Attach the poems to the rubbings and display them in an attractive grouping.

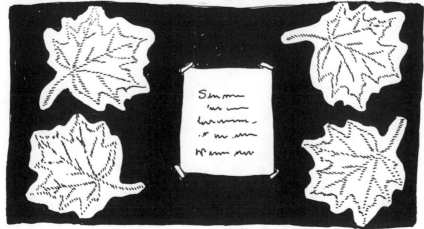

Winter Trees

READY

The lonely, barren trees of winter are perfect subjects for solemn cinquains. This writing activity will enable students to produce wonderful winter verses.

SET

Let the class go outside to observe the barren, winter trees. Allow the students to see, touch, feel, and explore every dimension of the trees.

WRITE

Copy the cinquain pattern below on the board or give a copy of the pattern to each student. Have the class brainstorm to make a list of all of the characteristics of winter trees. Instruct the students to include every sense impression they experienced while outside.

line 1	*tree*	(title)
line 2	*barren, deserted*	(2 adj.)
line 3	*withstanding, braving, fighting*	(3 "ing" verbs)
line 4	*nature's soldier of winter*	(4-word thought)
line 5	*maple*	(synonym)

PRESENT

Provide the students with sheets of gray paper. Using chalk, each student may sketch a winter landscape (without trees) on the paper. Direct the class to add trees using "straw-blowing" art. First, each student must drop a spoonful of watery black tempera paint on the scene. Then, the student may blow through a straw to spread the paint into a tree form. After the paint dries, the students may copy their poems on their landscapes. Display the work for all to read and admire.

Winter Is . . .

READY

Everyone has a unique opinion of winter. This descriptive activity allows students to express their true feelings about winter. (Descriptive definitions are popular activities, even with the youngest novice!)

SET

As a class, brainstorm to make a list of things that happen in winter. Ask the students questions to stimulate ideas.

WRITE

Have each student select three to five winter occurrences about which to write a poem. Encourage the students to use many adjectives in order to broaden the appeal of their poems.

> *Winter is...*
> *little children sledding down snowy hills,*
> *giant snowmen guarding wintry neighborhoods,*
> *tiny birds searching hungrily for food.*

PRESENT

Have each student illustrate a winter scene on a 5" x 7" Manila sheet. Instruct the students to color their scenes with crayons. Each student may cut white tissue paper into a 5" x 7" sheet to paste over his or her scene. The tissue paper adds a snowy cover on which the student may copy the winter poem.

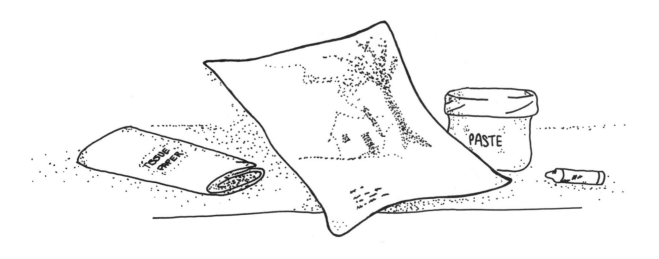

Snowflake Friends

READY

Snow-covered landscapes often have dreamy wonderland appearances. Let the magic of winter help to stretch students' imaginations.

SET

Ask the class to imagine that every snowflake is alive. Have the students compare the activities of snowflakes with the pastimes of friends. (Ask the students to think about how snowflakes play, run, sleep, etc.)

WRITE

Instruct the students to write about their snowflake friends, including what, where, and how the snowflakes "do" a specific activity.

Snowflake friends
hold hands in the wind
and run down hills
with terrific speed.

Snowflake friends
spend the night together
inside fluffy clouds
far above the ground.

PRESENT

Have the students design paper snowflake friends. Each student may glue several snowflakes on a sheet of construction paper and arrange them to form a body. The students may give their snowflake friends faces and arms with crayons. Ask the students to copy their poems on their designs. Hang the snowflake creations from the ceiling with string or display them on a winter bulletin board.

Penguins on Parade

READY

Young students will have fun preparing alliterative lines about these fun creatures of ice and snow.

SET

Read aloud an article on penguins or have the class view a film on penguins to familiarize the students with the appearance and activities of these winter birds.

WRITE

Have the class brainstorm all of the names and words beginning with the letter "P". Write the suggestions on the board. Instruct the students to write alliterative lines about penguins. Encourage the students to use their imaginations!

*Peter Penguin picks
playful pals with
whom to prance.*

*Patty Penguin
picnics with
purple people
and prickly
pelicans.*

*Paul Penguin
pins pink
petunias on
pretty people.*

PRESENT

Share the tongue-twisting "P" poems in an oral class presentation.

The students can also visually share their poems by creating construction paper penguins. Design a pattern or use one similar to the example below.

39

Winter Wardrobes

READY

People add pounds of clothing as winter months arrive. Writing about winter wardrobes can become quite vogue with students!

SET

On a chilly winter's day, have the class think about their winter wardrobes. Brainstorm together to make a list of winter attire and rhyming words. Write these lists on the board.

WRITE

A rhyming tercet is the perfect format to use for these carefree sketches. The rhyme patterns are as follows.

———— a	———— a	———— b	———— a
———— a	———— b	———— a	———— b
———— a	———— a	———— b	———— b

My pants are made of wool,   (a)
And my socks are, too,   (b)
My winter coat is the color blue!   (b)

PRESENT

Have the students make warmly dressed people on which to display their poems. Each student should fold a sheet of construction paper in half and cut out two large mitten shapes. Instruct the students to glue the two mittens together, thumbs out. Students may add paper circles for heads and crayon features to complete their figures. (Cotton may be attached for fur.) Have each student copy his or her poem on the mittens.

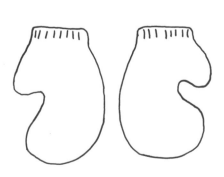

Winter "Breaks"

READY

Accidents are not the fondest memories of past winters, but they cause some "cracking" thoughts. Winter ice and bad weather often create the need for plaster casts. Help students turn winter accidents into positive experiences with this writing activity.

SET

Lead your class in a discussion about real experiences with broken bones. Perhaps there will be some firsthand experts in the class who may tell of their experiences. Talk about the sounds, feelings, appearances and other aspects of broken bones.

WRITE

Use the cinquain pattern as the framework for poems about winter accidents.

line 1	*ice*	(noun)
line 2	*slippery, dangerous*	(2 adj.)
line 3	*sliding, falling, crashing*	(3 "ing" verbs)
line 4	*crunch goes a bone*	(4-word phrase)
line 5	*help!*	(1 word)

PRESENT

Diagnose the students' verses with X-ray clarity! Direct the students to cut three to five shapes out of white paper to make a broken bone. Have the students glue the bone pieces in collage form on a sheet of black construction paper so that the fracture is obvious. Students may copy their poems below the broken bones.

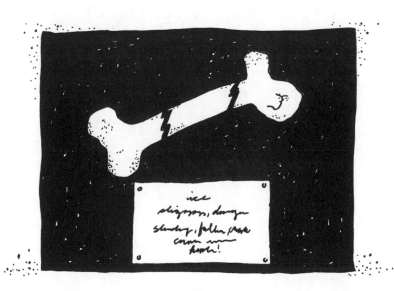

Snowmen's Vistas

READY

Snowmen are wintry sentinels who do nothing but observe the world around them. Students will enjoy looking through the eyes of a snowman and writing about what they see!

SET

Have the class brainstorm to make a list of everything a snowman might see on a winter day.

WRITE

Students may create wonderful winter verses using the "fill-in" poem model below. This is an excellent activity for building verb vocabularies.

line 1   A snowman stands so very still
line 2   He spies a (noun) on the hill
line 3   The (same noun)
line 4   (verb)   (verb)   (verb) and (verb).

A snowman stands so very still
He spies a squirrel on the hill
The squirrel
Scampers, scurries, leaps, and lands.

PRESENT

Have the students make snowmen portraits to accompany their snowmen poems. Each student may glue cotton balls on construction paper to make a snowman. Fabric scraps may become hats, scarfs, and shawls. Buttons and raisins may become eyes, noses, and mouths. Attach the poems to the snowmen and display the finished products for all to see.

Winter Waltz

READY

When the winter wind picks up its maestro's wand, one can see snowflakes dancing to the wind's symphonic sounds. Let this dazzling image of a winter snowstorm inspire students to write about the snowflake's dance.

SET

Read a story about a snowstorm to the class, or allow the students to talk about snowstorms they have heard about or experienced. Have the class make a list of action words to describe the movements of snowflakes. List adjectives to identify the appearance of each lacy flake.

WRITE

A lantern pattern provides the perfect framework for poems about the dance of the snowflake.

line 1	*twist* (action command)	(1 syllable)
line 2	*snowflake* (snowflake)	(2 syllables)
line 3	*up above* (where it is)	(3 syllables)
line 4	*a winter show* (description)	(4 syllables)
line 5	*spin* (action command)	(1 syllable)

PRESENT

Have the students make snowflake designs to accompany their poems. Instruct the students to cut snowflake designs out of white Styrofoam trays. Each student should add silver glitter to a snowflake and glue the snowflake on a sheet of black construction paper. The students may attach their poems to their snowflake designs and display them on a bulletin board, door, or wall.

W-W-Wind

READY

When the chilling winter gusts give way to warm and gentle wisps, spring has arrived. Whirl the class into spring with this fun alliterative activity.

SET

Ask the class to contribute as many **w** and **wh** words as they can to a list on the board. Tell the students to include lots of descriptive words and phrases.

WRITE

Ask each student to write a poem about the spring breezes using as many **w** and **wh** words as possible. The style, length, and content of each poem may vary.

Welcome, spring winds,
Whirling and whizzing,
Wisking and winding.
Welcome!

The warm wind
Whistles and whispers
Of wonderful weather to come.

PRESENT

Let the class make a musical wind mobile! After attaching tin can lids to a branch with fishing line, the students may copy their poems on pieces of construction paper and glue them to the lids. Hang the mobile outside the classroom window and listen to the spring breezes blow.

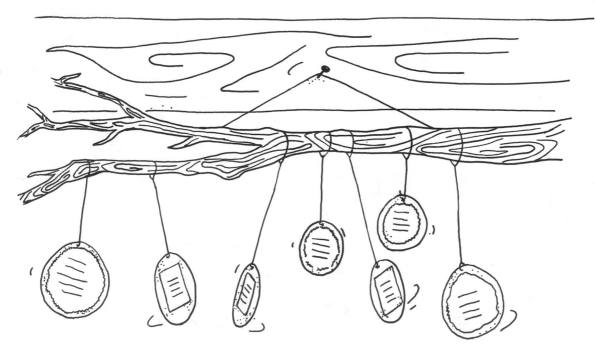

Spring Things

READY

Spring is the season of renewed promise and new growth. It is a perfect time to introduce the class to the more advanced metaphorical poem patterns. Mystical metaphors are springtime challenges that are sure to promote enthusiastic endeavors.

SET

"Regular" metaphors clearly state a comparison in the poem's first line. Mystical metaphors leave the reader guessing about what object the verse is describing.

WRITE

Have the class brainstorm to make a list of springtime things (jonquils, tulips, chicks, rain, sunshine, kites, picnics, etc.). Allow each student to select one spring thing for a poem topic. Instruct the writers to describe their objects in metaphorical form without mentioning the object's name.

Silver teardrops
Piercing puffs of white
Leave moistness in their path

PRESENT

Have the students illustrate their spring things using watercolors. After the paint dries, the students may copy their poems on their illustrations.

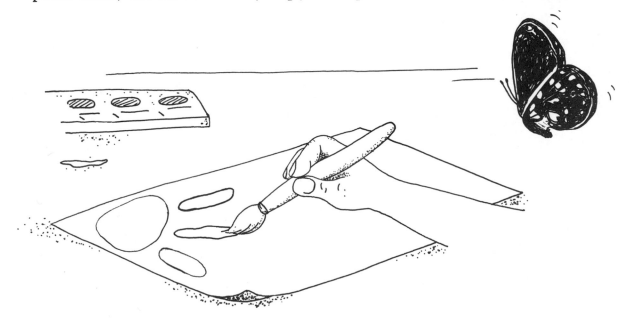

Dear Mother Nature

READY

Mother Nature is never busier than she is in spring. She ushers in warming winds, gentle rains, and sunny skies. She awakens flowers, trees, and animals. Have students write quizaines about Mother Nature's many tasks.

SET

A quizaine is a syllabic poem which consists of 15 syllables and which includes three lines of (7, 5, 3,) syllables respectively. The first line makes a statement. The remaining two lines ask a question.

WRITE

Help the class gather springtime thoughts in a brainstorming session after a nature walk. Ask each student to write a poetical question addressed to Mother Nature.

line 1	*Tender buds of springtime new,*	(7 syllables)
line 2	*Will Mother Nature*	(5 syllables)
line 3	*Water You?*	(3 syllables)

PRESENT

Cut large question marks out of brightly colored construction paper. Have each student decorate a question mark with spring art. The students may copy their poems on their question marks and mount the question marks on colorful backgrounds.

Sky Diamonds

READY

When the warm winds of spring begin to blow, fanciful "diamonds" appear in the sky. Capitalize on this favorite spring activity by allowing your students to make poetical kites!

SET

A diamante' is a diamond-shaped poem which builds a dynamic contrast between two opposite ideas or objects. Because its form demands a knowledge of the parts of speech, this activity is best suited for more capable writers.

WRITE

Review the diamante' form with the class. Make sure that the students understand the importance of line 4. This line ends the description of the first opposite and begins the description of the second opposite. Ask each student to select two opposite ideas or objects about which to write a diamante'.

line 1	*spring*	(topic)
line 2	*fresh, new*	(2 adj.)
line 3	*budding, growing, greening*	(3 "ing" verbs)
line 4	*blossoms, seedlings, fruits, compost*	(4 nouns)
line 5	*decaying, browning, dying*	(3 "ing" verbs)
line 6	*old, worn*	(2 adj.)
line 7	*fall*	(opposite)

PRESENT

Have the students make construction paper kites with crepe paper tails. Each student may copy his or her poem in the center of a kite and illustrate the opposites around the poem. Hang the kites in the room.

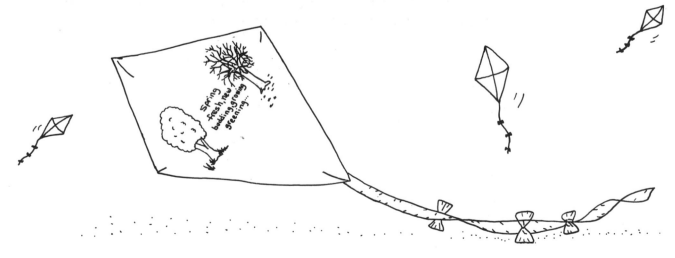

Spring Sings

READY

The sweet song of a bird, a sign that good weather is approaching, is a very familiar sound in spring. Have the class write about other ways that spring "sings".

SET

Lead a brainstorming session in which students try to name all of the activities that begin or occur in spring. Include natural happenings, plans, events, etc.

WRITE

Give each student a copy of this poem model to use as a guide in writing an original spring poem.

line 1	Spring sings with...
lines 2-4	(adj.) (noun) (action) (adv.)

Spring sings with...
Baby colts galloping down the lane,
Yellow chicks pecking in the field,
Soft winds whistling in the trees.

PRESENT

Give each student a sheet of blue construction paper. Instruct the students to draw large tree trunks with at at least one horizontal branch on their papers. Using shredded crepe paper or newspaper, each student may build a nest in the branch. Direct the students to drop four cotton balls into a paper sack filled with two or three tablespoons of powdered tempera paint. After shaking the bags to color the cotton, each student may glue two cotton balls in a nest to make a bird. Features may be added with paper scraps or crayons. Have the students attach their poems to their papers.

🌢 Rain Cinquains 🌢

READY

Rain showers are another springtime treat. Try to present this activity on a rainy day so that the dripping, splashing, and pounding of the rain will help inspire students to write wonderful rain poems.

SET

As the class listens to the rain, have them name all of the sounds they hear. Write a list of these words on the board.

WRITE

Familiarize the class with the adapted cinquain pattern below. Ask each student to write a rain cinquain.

line 1	*rain*	(noun)
line 2	*soft, cold*	(2 adj.)
line 3	*drip, drop, splash*	(3 sounds)
line 4	*fogs up my glasses*	(4-word phrase)
line 5	*rain*	(noun)

PRESENT

Make a "reading in the rain" bulletin board on which to display the poems. Cover the board with dark blue paper and glue construction paper raindrops on the board. Have each student cut out an umbrella and decorate it, leaving room in the center of the umbrella for a rain poem. Arrange the umbrellas on the board to create a colorful display.

Dandy Dandelions

READY

Dandelions are abundant in spring and are great stimuli for poetic endeavors. Collect an array of dandelions and prepare for an illuminating activity!

SET

Ask the class to examine the bouquet of dandelions and to name all of the characteristics of the flowers (size, shape, color, texture, aroma, etc.).

WRITE

Instruct each student to write a verse, using a simile format, that will detail for others the various qualities of a dandelion.

My dandelion is...
As round as the sun,
As soft as a pillow,
And as yellow as a lemon.

My dandelion is...
As wild as a lion,
As tame as a cat,
And as quiet as me.

PRESENT

Present the poems with dandelion art. Give each student a sheet of construction paper, crayons, glue, and two yellow cupcake papers. Instruct the students to trim 3/4 inch off of one cupcake paper and to draw a lion's face on the paper. After gluing the lion's face in the second cupcake paper, each student may glue the paper flower on a sheet of construction paper. Students may add stems and leaves with crayons. Have the students write their poems beside their dandelions.

Beautiful Butterflies

READY

One of nature's most beautiful creatures is the butterfly. The magnificent wings of this insect are sure to inspire students to write magnificent poems!

SET

If possible, capture a butterfly for the class to examine. (Keep the butterfly in a glass container!) Otherwise, students may observe pictures and mounted samples.

WRITE

Ask the students to brainstorm to make a list of the pretty, colorful, and beautiful things in the world. Write the following questions on the board and ask each student to answer one of these questions by writing a poem. Give the class several examples.

What is as pretty as a butterfly's wings?
What is as colorful as a butterfly's wings?
What is as beautiful as a butterfly's wings?

What is as pretty as a butterfly's wings?
A lacy skirt,
A red, red rose,
And a painting of the sea.

PRESENT

A fanciful butterfly art project will display the poems beautifully. Direct each student to draw the "body" of a butterfly on construction paper. Have the students make wings for their butterflies by gluing wadded tissue balls around their butterfly "bodies". The students may copy their poems on their butterfly creations.

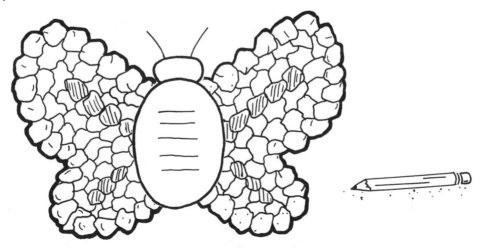

SUMMER

What fun it is to swim
Amid the green & blue
I'd like to be a fish
And splash around
with you.

Afternoons at the pool
Baseball games
Camping with my family
Dancing lessons
Eating strawberries

My T-shirt is from
summer camp.
Hiking in the hills,
Listening to ghost stories,
Sitting by the campfire.
I had a terrific summer.

Vacation Alphabet

READY

Let the class have fun alphabetizing their summer vacations!

SET

Give each student a decorative ditto sheet with the alphabet printed vertically on the left margin. Have the class brainstorm words or phrases that begin with the letters Q , X and Y.

WRITE

Ask each student to write a word or phrase describing his or her vacation for each letter of the alphabet.

Afternoons at the pool
Baseball games
Camping with my family
Dancing lessons
Eating strawberries

PRESENT

Give each student a construction paper letter of the alphabet. Instruct the students to decorate their letters according to the ideas listed in their vacation writings. Decorate a wall, board, or study area with the letters.

Summer Quintets

READY

Quintets lend themselves well to descriptions of carefree summer days. Students will enjoy reliving their summer memories as they write summer quintets.

SET

Have the class share ideas about summer memories and summer fun. Make a list of words and phrases on the board.

WRITE

The quintet is a syllabic verse form with (3,5,7,9,3) syllables to each line respectively. Encourage the students to spend time searching for the right word to fill each syllable requirement. Give each student a copy of the quintet pattern to use as a guide for writing an original summer quintet.

line 1	*sunset's glow*	(3 syllables)
line 2	*bright colored ribbons*	(5 syllables)
line 3	*shine in the evening's twilight*	(7 syllables)
line 4	*a picture painted in vibrant hue*	(9 syllables)
line 5	*magestic*	(3 syllables)

PRESENT

Let the students help make a banner to display their summer quintets. Have each student creatively illustrate his or her poem on drawing paper using crayons, markers, paint, chalk, or other materials. Glue the illustrations in an attractive arrangement on a long strip of butcher paper. Label the banner "summer fun" and fly it high for all to see!

Strawberry Fields

READY

One of summer's treats is a scrumptious strawberry. This activity will surely produce "tasty" verses!

SET

Bring strawberries to class and let the students study them. Ask the class to make a list of the characteristics of the berries. Write the words on the board to create a readily available word bank. (Allow the students to eat the strawberries!)

WRITE

Give each student a copy of the cinquain model below. Emphasize the importance of "taste" words.

line 1	strawberry	(noun)
line 2	luscious, sweet	(2 adj.)
line 3	satisfies, pleases, tempts	(3 verbs)
line 4	wonderful fruit of summer	(4-word phrase)
line 5	strawberry	(noun)

PRESENT

Have each student create a large recipe card on which to write his or her poem. (Provide one or more examples.) Students may decorate their cards with construction paper strawberries.

Bubble Gum Fun

READY

Kids love to chew bubble gum any time, but especially in the summertime. Capture the enthusiastic spirit possessed by most bubble gum chewers with this activity!

SET

Treat the class to a bubble gum break! As the students chew gum, make a class list of all-time favorite pastimes.

WRITE

This is a simple but fun writing activity. The first line of the poem should be this question: What's more fun than bubble gum? The next three lines should answer that question.

What's more fun than bubble gum?
Having a birthday party,
Going to a movie,
Eating ice cream.

PRESENT

Let the students make paper bubble gum machines on which to write their poems. Provide the class with pictures of bubble gum machines for reference. Encourage original designs!

Fishbowl Fantasies

READY

Summer's heat never annoys a fish, fluttering about in its cool, aquatic home. This writing activity will capture the wonder of such a water-bound existence.

SET

Bring a fishbowl with one or more fish to class for the students to observe. Discuss the characteristics of the fish such as size, shape, color, activity, etc.

WRITE

Review the quatrain verse form with the class. Have each student write a quatrain about what it would be like to be a fish.

> *What fun it is to swim,*
> *Amid the green and blue.*
> *I'd like to be a fish,*
> *And splash around with you.*

PRESENT

Instruct the students to cut fishbowls out of construction paper. Using tempera paint, each student may paint objects inside the bowl such as seaweed, rocks, sunken treasure chests, etc. Let each student cut a fish shape from a sponge, dip the sponge fish in paint, and press the sponge fish all over the bowl. When the paint dries, each student may copy his or her poem on the bowl. Have the students cover their fishbowls with plastic wrap for a glass effect.

60

T-shirt Vacations

READY

T-shirts are perfect attire for summer weather, and they're great for telling everyone where a vacation was spent. Have students use this advertising device to "sell" their favorite summer vacation spots.

SET

Conduct a class survey to find out where the students spent their summer vacations. Have each student list three to five activities that he or she participated in while on vacation.

WRITE

Give each student a copy of the fill-in poem model below. After reviewing the model, ask each student to fill in the blank to write an original poem which "sells" his or her vacation.

line 1	My T-shirt is from (place) _____ .
line 2-4	_____ (participle phrase) _____ .
line 5	I had a terrific summer!

My T-shirt is from summer camp.
Hiking in the hills,
Listening to ghost stories,
Sitting by the campfire.
I had a terrific summer!

PRESENT

Suspend a clothesline across the classroom. Let each student design a paper T-shirt to hang on the line. Have the students copy their poems on their shirts before hanging them on the line.

HOLIDAYS

When is Halloween?

READY

Every child knows when Halloween is — it's one of children's favorite occasions. Capitalize on students' Halloween excitement with this creative writing activity.

SET

Have the class make three lists of Halloween nouns, verbs, and adjectives. Write the word lists on the board and number the nouns column 1, the verbs column 2, and the adjectives column 3.

WRITE

Give each student a copy of the coded poem model below. Instruct the students to choose words from the appropriate columns to write original Halloween poems.

line 1	When is Halloween?		
line 2	When ____ (3)	(1)	(2)
line 3	And ____ (3)	(1)	(2)
line 4	When ____ (3)	(1)	(2)
line 5	And ____ (3)	(1)	(2)
line 6	Then it's Halloween!		

When is Halloween?
When spooky skeletons rattle,
And ghostly shadows lurk,
When wicked witches cackle,
And golden jack-o'-lanterns shine,
Then it's Halloween!

PRESENT

Have the students make and decorate October calendar pages. Instruct the students to decorate each day with a Halloween "figure", marking the 31st in some special way. Have each student write his or her poem at the top of the calendar page.

Ghostly Tales

READY

Teaching children conversational writing is often a tedious chore. Make this important writing skill fun to practice and easy to learn by allowing students to write ghostly tales.

SET

Conduct a brief lesson on the rules of conversational writing. (Include the uses of quotation marks.)

WRITE

Ask each student to pretend that he or she has just met a ghost. Have the students write the conversations that followed their ghostly meetings. Give each student a copy of the "fill-in" poem model below to use as a guide in writing a conversation. (Increase the complexity and length of the model according to the ages and capabilities of the students.)

line 1   One day I met a ghost.
line 2   The ghost was   (adj.) , (adj.) , and (adj.) .
line 3   The ghost said, "_____."
line 4   "_____," I said.
line 5   Then I _____.

One day I met a ghost.
The ghost was slim, spooky, and white.
The ghost said, "You're as pale as a sheet!"
"I've never seen a real ghost before," I said.
Then I turned and ran all the way home.

PRESENT

Have the class make portraits of their ghostly friends. Instruct each student to glue two buttons on a sheet of construction paper to make eyes. After dipping a piece of yarn in diluted glue, the student may place the yarn on the paper to outline a ghost's form. Have the students write their poems on their ghost portraits. Display the portraits in a reading center or on a bulletin board.

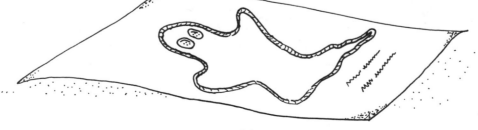

Turkey Tales

READY

When most people think of Thanksgiving, they think of eating turkey. Turn the tables this Thanksgiving and have students write about the holiday from the turkey's point of view!

SET

An alliterative verse will produce some Thanksgiving tongue twisters. Have the class make a list of nouns, adjectives, adverbs, and verbs beginning with the letter "T" that could be used to write a turkey "tale".

WRITE

Instruct the students to write some tongue twisters about Tom Turkey's terrifying Thanksgiving!

Tomorrow is Thanksgiving, and in turkey terms it's time for tragically treacherous terminations and totally terrible transactions.

Tradition tells Tom Turkey to tread on tiptoe when Thanksgiving transpires.

PRESENT

Have the class create some unique birds to accompany their tongue twisters. Provide the class with assorted materials such as seeds, buttons, magazines, newspapers, paper plates, construction paper, crayons and markers, etc. Instruct each student to draw a turkey and give it feathers and features using the assorted materials.

Have a class contest to see who can say his or her tongue twister the fastest!

Thankful Verses

READY

Thanksgiving is a time for reflecting upon our many blessings. Have students express their thankfulness with this reflective verse activity.

SET

Let the students discuss all of the things for which they are thankful. (Include persons, pets, belongings, talents, etc.)

WRITE

Present the reflection verse patterns below to the class. Have each student fill in the blanks to write an original verse.

Line 1   I give thanks for...
Lines 2-4   my   (adj.)   (noun)   ...   (why thankful)

I give thanks for...
my loving mother...she helps me,
my little sister...she gives me hugs,
my funny grandmother...she makes me laugh.

PRESENT

Have the students draw large turkeys without tail feathers on construction paper. Instruct each student to trace his or her hand on construction paper several times. After cutting out the turkey and hand prints, each student should glue the hand prints behind the turkey to make feathers. Have each student copy the first line of his or her poem on the turkey's body and each of the other lines on one of the "feathers". Group the turkeys in an attractive display.

Christmas Gifts

READY

Christmas is a gift-giving season. Give the class a fun alliterative writing activity which will spread the giving spirit throughout the classroom!

SET

Let the class spend a few minutes of informal sharing time. Allow each student to tell the class one gift that he or she would like which begins with the first letter in his or her name. (Keep a list on the board.)

WRITE

Write the following poem pattern on the board for the students to use as a guide in writing alliterative Christmas wishes.

Dear Santa,
 Please give _____ a _____ ,
 And _____ a _____ .
 Give _____ a _____ ,
 And _____ a _____ .
 As for me, I would like _____ .

Dear Santa,
 Please give Sally a sweater,
 And Wade a watch.
 Give Robbie a robot,
 And Debbie a doll.
 As for me, I would like a motorcycle!

PRESENT

Have each student cut package shapes out of wallpaper samples or wrapping paper. Instruct the students to tie their packages with ribbon and to write their poems on pieces of paper made to look like gift tags. Attach the poems to the packages. Use the packages to create an attractive holiday bulletin board, or allow the students to take their packages home.

Christmas Colors

READY

The world is filled with holiday color during the Christmas season. Descriptive verses about the colors of Christmas are lots of fun to write and share!

SET

Have the class make a list of colors that can be used to describe the Christmas season. Remind students not to limit themselves to red and green. Keep a list on the board.

WRITE

Present this poem model as a writing guide for the class. Students may use this form to write descriptive verses, or they may create their own verse forms.

line 1   My favorite Christmas <u>color is   (color)</u>   ...
lines 2-4   <u>(same color)   as   (what and where)</u>

My favorite Christmas color is blue...
Blue as the eyes of a jolly little elf,
Blue as the gown on a treetop angel,
Blue as the ribbon on a wrapped package.

PRESENT

Let each student make a Christmas hand print wreath using the color theme of his or her poem. Instruct each student to draw a 6" circle on a large sheet of butcher paper. After dipping a hand in tempera paint, the student should then place the hand palm down on the circle's edge, continuing in this way all around the circle. After the paint dries, the student may cut around the hand print border. Students may attach their poems to their colorful wreaths with ribbon.

Quick Saint Nick

READY

Santa is said to enter and leave each home on Christmas Eve as quickly as the wink of an eye. Have the class imitate his speed as they write couplets about Saint Nick.

SET

Lead a class brainstorming session about Santa. Make lists of words for Santa's equipment, preparations, appearance, etc.

WRITE

Write the following poem model on the board for students to use in writing couplet rhymes about Santa. Remind the students that the words at the end of each line must rhyme!

line 1   Santa's (noun) is (description) _____ ,

line 2   _____ (expand description) _____ .

Santa's sleigh is filled with toys,
For lots of little girls and boys.

Santa's suit is very red,
Like the quilt upon my bed.

PRESENT

These brief jingles require a simple art project. Have the students make Santas using only construction paper circles and triangles. Let the students write their couplets on construction paper "goodie bags" which may be attached to the Santas.

70

Reindeer Rhymes

READY

You know Dasher and Dancer and Prancer and Vixen, but do you know Fred, Ron, Hank and Harry? These are reindeer who tried to make Santa's team but failed. Students will have fun creating limericks about the mishaps of these reindeer!

SET

Have the class brainstorm to make a list of all the qualities a reindeer must have to be selected for Santa's team. Have the class review the limerick form and write some preliminary limericks before beginning their reindeer rhymes.

WRITE

Instruct each student to invent a reindeer name and to write about the reindeer's misfortune in limerick fashion. Provide the students with copies of the limerick model below.

line 1	*There once was a reindeer named* <u>Fred,</u>	(a)
	(name)	
line 2	*Who wanted to fly Santa's sled.*	(a)
	(what he/she did)	
line 3	*He jumped and he slid,*	(b)
	(what went wrong)	
line 4	*He scared every kid,*	(b)
	(what went wrong)	
line 5	*And Santa picked Dasher instead!*	(a)
	(result)	

PRESENT

Let the students illustrate their reindeer! Provide the students with a creative supply of art materials and encourage the students to use their imaginations. Display each reindeer beside the corresponding reindeer limerick.

The Little Things of Christmas

READY

Christmas, one of the biggest celebrations of the year, is often treasured most for its "little" pleasures. Have students elaborate on the little things that make Christmas' joy great.

SET

Have the class make a big list of the little things that make Christmas special. Write the list on the board.

WRITE

Have the students use the poem pattern below to write little poems about the little things of Christmas.

line 1   Christmas is for little things...
lines 2-4   (list the "little things")

Christmas is for little things...
A kiss for Grandma,
A smile for a friend,
A hug for Mom.

PRESENT

Let each student make a little elf to accompany his or her poem! Provide the students with pictures of elfs and/or encourage the students to create their own elfs. Instruct the students to copy their poems on construction paper packages. Display the elves and poems together.

Menorah Merriment

READY

Chanukah is an eight-day celebration centered around the lighting of a special candelabrum called a menorah. This writing activity will have students writing cinquains as they learn about this Jewish holiday.

SET

Familiarize the class with the history, traditions, and activities of Chanukah, the festival of lights. If possible, have a Jewish student or visitor share a personal account of the celebration. Bring a menorah to class for the students to observe.

WRITE

The light of the menorah breaks the darkness of the winter nights during Chanukah. Have the students use the cinquain poem model below to write about this bright beacon.

line 1	*menorah*	(topic)
line 2	*golden, sacred*	(2 adj.)
line 3	*reminding, glowing, shining*	(3 "ing" verbs)
line 4	*it warms our hearts*	(4-word phrase)
line 5	*twinkling torch*	(synonym, metaphorical phrase)

PRESENT

Spotlight the poems with a light-on-dark art project. Instruct the students to create winter night scenes using black construction paper and white chalk. Have the students glue yellow construction paper in the foregrounds of the scenes on which to write their poems.

Spinning Dreidel

READY

Chanukah is a time of wishes for good fortune. Have students join in the celebration of Chanukah by "spinning" joyful holiday poems about the dreidel game that is a Chanukah tradition.

SET

Bring a dreidel to class and explain the rules and purpose of the game. Allow the students to play the game.

WRITE

Give each student a copy of the poem model below. Lines 1 and 3 are constant. Instruct the students to write poems about the spinning dreidel.

line 1	*spin, dreidel, spin*
line 2	*like an autumn leaf falling*
line 3	*spin, dreidel, spin*
line 4	*bring fun to everyone*

PRESENT

Let the students make flat or three-dimensional paper dreidels. Attach the poems to the spinning tops and display them in an attractive grouping.

Anonymous Valentines

READY

Sending an anonymous valentine is lots of fun. This writing activity combines the spirit of Valentine's Day and the excitement of solving riddles to create an especially fun project.

SET

Many commercial valentines are written in riddle form. Collect several commercial valentines and bring them to class for the students to read. (You also might like to provide the class with riddle books.)

WRITE

Instruct each student to write a riddle describing himself or herself. The description should include personality traits and physical traits. Present the following riddle as an example. Each description must begin and end as the example below.

> *Guess who loves you.*
> *She's tall with hair like honey,*
> *She's sweet, but not too sweet,*
> *She has blue eyes,*
> *She smiles a lot,*
> *And she wears jeans almost every day.*
> *Give up? ... it's me!*

PRESENT

Have each student make several small construction paper hearts and glue them on a sheet of paper to form a question mark. Each student may copy his or her poem on or below the question mark. Collect the riddles, shuffle them well, and redistribute them to the students. Ask the students to try guessing the riddles!

Broken Hearts

READY

Valentine's Day is traditionally a celebration of love and happiness. This writing activity, however, will allow students to express their thoughts about the "other side of love" -- broken hearts.

SET

Read a story to the class about a "broken heart". Discuss how it feels to have a broken heart. Have the class list all of the situations or occurrences that could cause a heart to break.

WRITE

The appropriate verse form for broken heart poems will vary according to the grade level. The verses below are suitable models for kindergarten through third grade. Have the students write their own broken heart poems.

My heart broke
When I got sick
On my birthday.

My heart broke
When my puppy
Ran away.

PRESENT

Have the students make broken hearts on which to display their poems. Instruct each student to cut a heart out of red construction paper and to cut the heart into two halves. After gluing the broken heart on construction paper, each student may copy his or her poem on the broken heart. Students may decorate their broken heart projects with doilies, crayons, and markers.

The Leprechaun Legend

READY

An old legend says that if someone catches a leprechaun, the leprechaun will grant the person three wishes. Present this activity to celebrate St. Patrick's Day and the leprechaun legend.

SET

Let the students share their dreams and wishes with each other. Share yours with the class, too!

WRITE

Ask each student to choose three wishes to fill in the poem model below.

> If a leprechaun granted me three wishes,
> This is what they would be...
> A (1 syllable) , a (1 syllable) , and (3 syllables) ,
> These are my wishes three!

> *If a leprechaun granted me three wishes,*
> *This is what they would be...*
> *A dog, a bike, a baseball bat,*
> *These are my wishes three!*

PRESENT

Have the students make magic wands to present their poems. Instruct each student to roll a large, sturdy sheet of paper to make a tube. (Have the students tape or glue the tubes.) Instruct each student to cut a star out of yellow construction paper to attach to the end of the tube. Have the students cut three shamrocks each out of green construction paper to suspend from their stars with string. Direct each student to write the first two lines of the poem on the star and the three wishes on the shamrocks. Let the students take their St. Patrick's Day wands home.

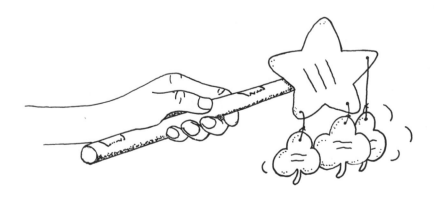

Easter Bunny Express

READY

For a great Easter writing activity, have the class write some "bouncing" verses describing the Easter bunny.

SET

For a fun warm-up, teach the class the bunny hop! Then, have the class brainstorm action words that describe the Easter bunny's movements. Also brainstorm adjectives that describe his appearance. Keep a list on the board.

WRITE

Review the cinquain form with the class. Write the cinquain pattern below on the board. Instruct the students to write cinquains about Easter's "mascot".

line 1	*Easter bunny*	(noun)
line 2	*fluffy, happy*	(2 adj.)
line 3	*wiggles, hops, thumps*	(3 verbs)
line 4	*delivers eggs by jumping*	(4-word phrase)
line 5	*Peter Cottontail*	(synonym or nickname)

PRESENT

Have the students make construction paper bunnies to accompany their poems. Provide the students with paper, glue, scissors, cotton, fabric, pipe cleaners, and other materials. Encourage the students to be creative. Students may copy their poems on their creations. Display the bunnies in a row for a bouncing bunny express!

Easter Riddles

READY

Every egg has a surprise within its shell, whether it be a chick, a duck, or simply a breakfast treat. Let the class write poems about special Easter eggs that contain special surprises!

SET

Provide each student with a plastic egg. Before class, put inside each egg a picture from a magazine or newspaper of a treat that the Easter Bunny might bring. Let each student open an egg to discover what surprise will be the subject of his or her poem.

WRITE

Give each student a copy of the riddle pattern below. Instruct the students to use the pattern to describe their surprises without naming them.

line 1	My Easter egg has a surprise inside,
line 2	it's ___(adj.)___ ,
line 3	it's ___(adj.)___ ,
line 4	it sometimes ___(hint)___ .
line 5	Is it still a surprise?

My Easter egg has a surprise inside,
   it's round,
   it's golden,
   it sometimes is worn on a finger.
Is it still a surprise?

My Easter egg has a surprise inside,
   it's bouncy,
   it's striped,
   it sometimes rolls into the street.
Is it still a surprise?

PRESENT

Let the students share their poems with the class. After the class makes three guesses, the student should open the egg to reveal the surprise. After all of the poems have been shared, display them on the wall just outside the room for passers-by to read and solve.